Right Relationships:

The Balancing Act

By **Joe Love**

CONTENT

Introduction

No matter how much money, status, professional success, or other types of external security one may have, very few people experience true joy and personal freedom. No matter how hard we try, our life always seems to be a little off-center and this seems to characterize life for most of us. Right relationships are the foundation for a successful, happy and fulfilling life. People will look to others to make them happy and move from relationship to relationship seeking answers only to entrap themselves in a never- ending circle of worry, anxiety, and uneasiness.

Jesus said, "The kingdom of Heaven is within you." Unless we understand this, we miss the opportunity to learn and grow from the people who come into our lives in fact, most people who come into our lives are divine teachers in disguise trying to point out the very thing we need to learn.

In this book, I'll share with you my insights, strategies and case studies from my own practice to help you understand how relationships work - why certain people come into your life, what to look for and how to get the most out of a relationship for you and the other person. You'll learn how the Universe deliberately brings people into our lives as divine teachers to help us. As an intuitive, spiritual teacher and author, I've devoted my life to helping individuals develop their sixth sense, use it to expand their awareness, and reconnect with their higher self, opening the pathway to their spirit. I look forward to helping you create better relationships and experience peace and joy flowing into every area of your life.

Chapter 1

Relationships: Redefining Soul Mate

When it comes to relationships, the number one question people ask me is about their soul mate. Often they've been in a challenging relationship and eventually look for something better, trying to find the right person.

There are two important misconceptions when it comes to soul mates. The first is that there is just one soul mate for each of us. The truth is we can have many in our lifetime because our soul mates are those people who come into our lives to teach us lessons and help us grow. The second misconception is that our soul mates are people who are exactly like us in almost every way.

In fact, it's just the opposite. Our soul mates are people who are different from us in so many ways. If they were exactly like us then they wouldn't be able to teach us the lessons we need to learn so we can grow. When we look for a mate or spouse, the natural tendency for us is to think of the other person in terms of "what do we have in common?" We usually think, if we have everything in common with the other person we have found our soul mate. Relationships like this rarely last long because this person is not your soul mate. You don't need more of what you already are. You should not be looking for a mirror of yourself.

Being at peace is at the essence of feeling whole. It is the essence of spiritual growth. Any moment you are at peace, you are in an enlightened state with your higher self. All people have peaceful thoughts but the difference between an enlightened person and one who is not is the enlightened person does not have judgment, anger, fear or anxiety.

These are all emotions most people have come to believe is a normal part of our lives. Look at the people who come into our lives who know how to push our buttons, such as your in-laws, a co-worker but most often it is our spouse or our children. When these people show up in our lives they can take us away from our peace. These people are your soul mates because they are teaching you valuable lessons you need to learn to become whole.

They are teaching, you haven't mastered yourself and you are not in charge of yourself yet. Think, if we have everything in common with the other person we have found our soul mate. Relationships like this rarely last long because this person is not your soul mate. You don't need more of what you already are. You should not be looking for a mirror of yourself.

Being at peace is at the essence of feeling whole. It is the essence of spiritual growth. Any moment you are at peace, you are in an enlightened state with your higher self. All people have peaceful thoughts but the difference between an enlightened person and one who is not is the enlightened person does not have judgment, anger, fear or anxiety. These are all emotions most people have come to believe is a normal part of our lives. Look at the people who come into our lives who know how to push our buttons, such as your in-laws, a co-worker but most often it is our spouse or our children. When these people show up in our lives they can take us away from our peace. These people are your soul mates because they are teaching you valuable lessons you need to learn to become whole. They are teaching, you haven't mastered yourself and you are not in charge of yourself yet.

These people who can push your buttons and make you angry are really divine masters disguised as manipulative, crass, unconcerned people. Rather than getting angry at these people and trying to change them or get away from them you should be appreciating them and looking for what they are trying to teach you. These people may be your in-laws, parents, or co-workers but most often, it's your spouse or children.

You may succeed in getting them out of your life but then if you haven't learned the lessons they were trying to teach you then you will attract the same type of people back into your life in some type of relationship, romantic, work or other and the cycle begins all over again until the lessons are learned.

We fight this because our ego wants us to be right, have all the answers, and be in control of everything, whereas our higher self simply wants peace.

This is what relationships are meant to teach us, to become whole, to be at peace with ourselves and enjoy life. As author and inspirational speaker Dr. Wayne Dyer so often says: "When you have the choice to be right or be kind always choose to be kind." When you do this you are honoring your higher self and letting go of your ego.

Once you learn that the people in your life whom you are in conflict with or have difficulty with, whether it's someone who is alive or someone who has passed on, know you can always choose peace in the relationship. Once you learn to do this you will know the reason these people have come into your life is to teach you how to grow, become whole and honor your higher self. They are teachers like you are to others.

You have to let go of the ego-driven need to constantly be proving yourself and making yourself right and even in some cases to make the other person wrong. If you feel the need to put someone down, don't say anything at all. Practice this with everyone, not only in your close personal relationships but with anyone you meet.

Chapter 2

Recognizing Relationship Patterns

Look for relationships patterns that have repeated over and over again in your life, at work, at home and with friends. Patterns we continue to experience are what we need to learn. Step back and ask yourself, "What is it I need to learn from these patterns?" It's not that we have to keep experiencing the same thing over and over again for no reason. Instead, there are lessons to be learned in all of our relationships. So take a moment to consider some of the patterns in your relationships that have repeated themselves throughout your life.

Rather than see yourself as a victim, see yourself as an individual who is dealing with memories and experiences within yourself that are coming to the surface so you can deal with them, heal them, and then transform them. When you have the opportunity, take ten to fifteen minutes and write down some of the patterns that you have repeatedly experienced in your relationships. Sit back and look at those patterns. See if there is something you can learn about yourself by having gone through those experiences.

If you don't see anything you can learn, ask a friend for his or her advice on why you keep having the same experiences over and over again in your relationships. What is the lesson there you can learn? Sometimes getting objective feedback from others can be valuable.

Chapter 3

Personal Relationships

Part of our challenges with relationships is we were brought up with stories and fairy tales such as "Sleeping Beauty", Beauty and the Beast", and "Cinderella" which always had a happy ending. No one ever told us as children what really comes after "happily ever after" - life is more challenging than we desire it to be. For example, I had a client whom I had been working with for some time. She was married and had two young children.

The woman came to me for an intuitive reading because she had just met another man who she felt was her true soul mate. I tried to explain to her we have many soul mates, not one.

In doing the reading, I could see her husband was her soul mate just as this other man whom she had recently met was. There were important lessons both men were there to teach her. I did not see any problems in her current marriage that could not be worked out and I gave her suggestions that came through during the reading from her spirit guides as to how to make the relationship better.

She wouldn't hear of it. In her mind, this new man she met was her true soul mate, the man of her dreams, so she made the decision to divorce her husband to live with this other man and within six months they were separated and she was on a downward spiral which took her a very long time to recover from. Very often what happens in our relationships is people come into our lives to help us bring the issues, experiences, and challenges we have to work on to the forefront. One of the biggest challenges is very often most of us feel "If he or she really loved me they would change" but you should counter that with "If he or she really loved me they would accept me the way I am." Many people have ironic understandings of how relationships work and this is what causes a lot of difficulties.

Chapter 4

Learning the Lessons

If there is one Universal lesson we need to learn and teach our children, it is oneness. Somehow, we are all connected at a very deep level. We share our soul journey with everyone on the planet. If you want to know if you have a soul mate relationship with someone all you need to look at is the kind of emotional connection you have with the person. Any person who we have a very strong emotional connection, positive or negative, is our soul mate.

Let's say for example, you have a boss at work that is very demanding and expects a lot from you, even if you leave the job at some point the same type of person is likely to be with you at your next job or show up somewhere else in your life. There is never going to be a perfect relationship and once you find it you'll be happy.

All relationships have the potential to be a purposeful and happy experience in terms of soul growth and personal transformation. Sometimes this works because someone provokes us, pushes all of our buttons, someone helps us to uncover talents and abilities deep inside ourselves we didn't know we had, or simply being around that person challenges us to do something differently.

Relationships can be a very hard growth experience but ultimately even our most difficult ones can help us become a better person. The Universe very often puts the same people together because they are working on a similar lesson. Often husbands and wives will tell each other what the other person should be working on in their relationship but that does not make for a healthy relationship.

Instead you should be sitting down at least once a month with your partner and be open and honest about the difficulties you are having. You should be asking for help from each other on how to solve these problems and difficulties. This is a wonderful way to help each other grow and foster a closer, more loving and happier relationship.

We learn the most about ourselves through our interactions with others. People in our lives act like a mirror and any time we have an emotional response to another person, be it positive or negative, we see a part of ourselves and that is what we are responding to.

In fact, it's impossible to have an emotional response to another person and not see a part of ourselves. For example, if someone you admire really inspires you or brings out the best in you, it's because you're seeing an aspect of yourself.

Perhaps you haven't worked on the ability or quality to develop it but the reason you have such an emotional connection to the other person is because it's a part of you. Conversely, if someone in your life really bothers you, for example a person walks into the room and you feel anger, the same is true you are seeing a part of yourself in that person you need to work on.

All of us hope that any irritating qualities we may have are not as obvious as they are in another person. It's important to understand even your worst enemy has a best friend and even your best friend has someone who doesn't like him or her. The reason this is true is because we are conditioned to see other people as a mirror.

In my workshops and individual consultations, I often tell people to look at the people in their life who bother them, or those who seem to really get under their skin and drive them crazy because they will be able to see their own strengths and weaknesses in those people.

As souls seeking personal wholeness, our intention is to eventually learn how to love everyone with whom we come in contact with. In the Bible, Romans 2:11 there is a verse many people overlook, "God is no respecter of persons." I believe this to mean that God loves us all equally. For example, God loves the coworker you cannot stand as much as He loves you.

Ultimately, all relationships have the potential to be purposeful and helpful experiences in terms of soul growth and personal transformation. The challenge would be if you are looking for the perfect relationship to find your one and only soul mate, someone to make you happy and this is usually the goal for most people. Instead you should be looking for someone to help you become whole.

This is a different goal because most people set out to find someone who will make them happy. This is the critical part of having a happy and fulfilling relationship most people miss because they don't understand it is wholeness our spirit really desires. It is why we are on this earth.

Ultimately, we all return to our awareness of oneness with God but we are never done until every person achieves the same oneness. For example, think about the most troubled person you know. Until that person is whole you are not done either. I have many people ask me why they can't find the one perfect person to spend their life with or they are in a relationship and want to know if the person they are with is their soul mate.

When clients come to me with relationship questions, during the reading I often see the person my client is in a relationship with could be their soul mate but ultimately the relationship will be what they choose it to be. In a relationship, you will not always be happy but the conditions between you and the other person are always there to enable you both to become compatible, content and help each other grow. I will often remind clients that any relationship is ultimately a 50/50 proposition.

What I mean by this is in any relationship you need to have a unity of purpose in what you and your partner are trying to accomplish. For any relationship to work you have to watch out for self-interests irrespective of the other. In other words, beware of selfishness. For example, I had a client who came to me for an intuitive reading. She had been dating this man for many years and felt they knew each other so well it was a given he was her soul mate and they were perfect for each other.

During the reading, I could see there were a lot of issues from their past neither had learned and I could see she didn't know him as well as she thought. I could see many control issues with him that had yet to come to the surface and she could not see them. I saw neither had even begun to learn the lessons needed to have a good marital relationship.

I told her that if they got married it would be very troubled and not last very long. She did not want to hear it and said what I was seeing was wrong. They got married and started fighting immediately about money, religion, and philosophy. He became very controlling as head of the household. It was as I had warned her to beware of issues from their past that were not yet learned or had healed.

After one year they were divorced. Sometimes we don't understand the lessons we're supposed to learn or what our karmic memory is trying to relate to us. For example, I had a client come to me for a consultation that had been brought up in a verbally abusive household where her mom, dad, and sister were always putting her down and criticizing her.

She got married and her husband became verbally abusive to her as well and would even belittle and embarrass her in front of others. As soon as her children could speak they would talk back to her and as they got older would even criticize her for not being a good mother. In her job, her boss and co-workers would criticize her for what she described as every little thing.

This is an important lesson. The Universe kept bringing to this woman people who had the same opinion of her as she did of herself. Until she raised her opinion about herself and raised her self-esteem the Universe was going to keep bringing people into her life that had the same opinion of her.

So as I explained to her, she didn't have to put up with these people in her life, rather she needed to change the way she thought about herself, which she eventually did and her life changed for the better.

The point here is sometimes we don't understand the lesson and this is especially true if the lesson keeps presenting itself over and over again. One of the most important lessons the Universe teaches us is never to be a doormat or to put up with negativity. If you see this happening, you have to change something in your life. Here's an exercise I have many of my clients do to help them better understand the lessons from a particular relationship:

Go to a peaceful spot in your home where there is no phone, computer or television, where you won't be disturbed. Sit quietly, close your eyes and breathe deeply in through the nose and out through the mouth. Now imagine a challenging or difficult relationship you had in the past. This could have been with a family member, friend or someone you worked with. Visualize how you felt when you were around this person. See if you can identify what the Universe was trying to teach you about yourself.

For example, was spirit trying to teach you to speak up for yourself; learn patience or learn unconditional love, or to eradicate negative patterns within yourself? This person was really trying to show you a number of things about yourself that can be very helpful in your life. What were they? What did you learn about yourself? Now, see if you can imagine a mutual intention you had with this person.

What could you have had in common with this person? Can you see this person the way God might see him or her? Could you see them as one of their family members sees them? Can you see their issues, struggles and problems? Could you forgive them? When you think of them, imagine what they were trying to teach you about yourself. The point of this exercise is to understand even the most challenging relationships have helped you to become who you are today.

A question I am asked frequently is "how can we keep our love alive in a troubled marriage?" To answer this question, you have to first define what love is. Love is giving. Love is growth. It must be cultivated. It must be shared and selflessness on the part of each is necessary. Love grows; love endures; love forgives; love understands.

Never sit still and expect the other person to do all the giving and all the forgiving, rather both partners need to complement each other, forever. Soul mates are not limited to male/female relationships. You can a have soul mate relationships with a friend, coworkers and children. It is any kind of relationships where you have an emotional connection to someone, good or bad. A soul mate is essentially an individual we draw toward ourselves in the present so we can learn from them through our experiences with one another.

Here's another exercise to help better understand what a specific relationship has taught you: Sit quietly in a place where you will not be disturbed or have any distractions. Close your eyes, breathe deeply, and picture an individual in your life you truly loved. It can be someone living or deceased. It could be a grandparent, parent, friend, sibling, relative, co-worker or a child.

Imagine the person is standing in front of you and recall the person's talents and strengths. Remember what it felt like to be in the presence of this person. How does the person make you feel? What qualities are most evident in this person through his or her actions and words? Is the person kind, loving, joyous? Now try to discover what it was this individual tried to teach you about yourself. Perhaps it was self-acceptance, how to be more loving and empathetic towards yourself, or discovering more joy and laughter with others.

It could have been all of these and more. This person tried to show you a number of qualities that would be helpful in life, what were they? Take some time and write down the qualities this person exhibited and why these qualities were admirable to you. The qualities about this person that most affected you are most likely a mirror of the qualities you possess within yourself. Perhaps you haven't worked on them to the same extent or maybe they are not yet evident to you.

The fact you were able to see them in another person and admire them are evidence you also possess these qualities. So take the time to acknowledge yourself and some of the positive aspects you have in your own life because we all have strengths and weaknesses but we tend to focus on what's wrong with us rather than what's right.

Chapter 5

Family Resources

Our families are there for a reason, a purpose, to help every member of the family become a better person. We are all evolving and growing, learning lessons, becoming a better person by being around the people in our families.

Many times our relationship with one of our family members is very challenging and we learn not to like the person or instead we learn how to gain a new awareness so we can help people who are like the person who has traits similar to the challenging person. Not everyone will become a better person because of the support of family members However, we can gain needed resources by being around them.

The Universe is very much involved in adoption and brings together souls exactly where they need to be. Very often people who were adopted have had the same type of past life connections. It works for everyone - friends, neighbors, and children. Once you love someone, love exists for eternity, but you need to adjust the situation for the present time.

For example, very often we're drawn to people who we've been with in a past life and we need to make it appropriate for the present life. Remember, we've all had relationships with spouses from the past. We often come into contact with past spouses not because the Universe wants us to pick those relationships up in the present but because once love exists, it exists forever.

Chapter 6

Law of Expectation

The Universal Law of Expectation says if you expect nothing out of life you will not be disappointed. Whatever you expect sets up a dynamic that will affect you, either positively or negatively. We can transform any relationship in our life ultimately because the person we are changing is ourselves. As we change, how we respond to other people changes and they in turn, will respond differently as well. When we perceive certain things in people, it is for our own benefit. We are observing qualities, aspects, or actions of other people so we can learn about ourselves.

Whatever we expect has a great deal to do with the outcome we experience. Every relationship can ultimately be a good and fulfilling experience. However sometimes there is a difference between being in a relationship for the long haul versus working through a short- term relationship so we can learn the lessons we need to learn in order to grow.

All relationships have lessons involved. For example, we try to emulate another person's qualities and capabilities while becoming a better person in our own right. On other occasions, we have to bring out the very best within us in order to deal with the other person.

How can you tell the difference between working with a relationship for the long haul versus working through a short-term relationship to simply learn the lessons you need to learn? Think of it in these terms.

Since the ultimate purpose of a relationship is to help you become whole, you need to ask yourself these questions; does this relationship make me a better person? Does it challenge or stretch me? Does it encourage me to become a more balanced and giving person? Does this relationship bring out the very best in me?

In order to maintain healthy relationships, we really need to ultimately be able to answer yes to all of those questions. If you're currently involved in a relationship where the answer to these questions is no, you can be sure there are lessons you need to learn. However, as you work on these lessons and transform your own perceptions, thereby transforming yourself in the process, you'll eventually be able to come back and answer yes to all these questions.

Chapter 7

Mindset for Marriage

In a marriage, it's often easier to tell your spouse what he or she needs to work on but, ultimately, soul growth and development is based on you working on your own lessons. During the process you may be able to assist your partner in mastering theirs. However, you should play the role of facilitator, not dictator. With this is mind, whenever you catch yourself concentrating on your partner's lessons, you need to stop and return your focus to what you are supposed to discover.

This will help you move forward in the relationship to assist your partner to learn whatever lesson he or she needs to learn. For example, in my consulting sessions with people who are having marital issues, I will often have the client imagine how his or her spouse would describe their ideal spouse.

How would his or her spouse say the other should act during the course of a day? What would an ideal spouse do? Once my client has answered these questions, I advise him or her to begin acting in that way and eventually he or she will bring out many of those same traits in their spouse.

This illustrates the importance of focusing on our own self in terms of what we do in our relationship with others and what we are trying to learn in the experience.

With this in mind I encourage you to make some lists:

Marriage: What would your spouse say his or her ideal partner would be like?

Business: What is your company's view of an ideal employee?

Parent: What would your children say their ideal parent would be like?

Friend: What would your friends say an ideal friend would be like?

Then begin assuming those roles and acting out those points on your list in order to transform yourself and become the best person you can be - the kind of person you were meant to be. We learn the most about ourselves through our interactions with others.

In my consulting practice, I deal with a lot of people who have relationship problems and I often hear clients say, "I've lived this way all my life, I can't change," or "This relationship has been going on this way for so many years, it'll never change". The most important truth about ourselves is we are always growing and learning and it is the people who come into our lives that help us to grow.

We learn most about ourselves through our interactions with others and because of this I use the analogy of "the mirror" when we meet people. Often, they are a mirror of what is going on inside of us. We draw to ourselves people who not only possess the same characteristics we have in terms of strengths but somehow, they push our buttons to pull out our weaknesses that we need to work on.

Philosopher, author and inspirational speaker, Dr. Wayne Dyer summed up attraction in relationships best, "We don't attract into our lives what we want, rather we attract what we are."

If we don't like the way things are going in our life and want our outside world to change, then we first have to change who we are inside.

People in our life act like a mirror. If you want to see what you need to work on look at the people in your life that irritate and rub you the wrong way. There are Universal Laws of Attraction and Effect. These two laws really pull together what we need to learn and why certain people are drawn to us by the Universe.

When having marriage troubles – constantly bumping up against each other, feeling like it is never going to work out and that divorce is the only answer – if we agree to keep working at it, not only can we make the marriage work but we both can become better people in the process and that's what it's really all about.

When having relationship problems and each person is faced with a mirror of themselves and each soul meets itself.

You have to understand the hardships we blame on our partner are really caused by ourselves.

Chapter 8

Loneliness

I am often asked, "If I have all these past relationships why am I so lonely? Why can't I find the right person?" Loneliness is due to two factors. Very often in life our spirit is trying to manifest something. It might be a talent or ability, or something the spirit really wants to do or needs but we often cut our spirit off by viewing life through our ego and intellect.

The ego will often say "You can't make enough money doing that, or you don't have enough talent to do that; you'll never be successful; you can't do it." When we disconnect from spirit and what it is trying to manifest outwardly, it manifests as loneliness because you have isolated yourself from who you really are. A divine spiritual being having a human experience.

Very often, we inadvertently cut ourselves off from someone in our surroundings who needs us to reach out and help them and it manifests as loneliness in us.

If you feel lonely, do an inventory: is there someone in your life you have inadvertently cut yourself off from? Or is there something you've always wanted to do and never let yourself be free and have the courage to do? If you are lonely and can address either of these, you won't feel lonely any longer.

As souls seeking personal wholeness, to reconnect with our spirit. Our intention is to eventually learn how to love everyone with whom we come into contact-even people who have personalities we don't like – if you look for their good qualities you will find them.

Keep in mind the "Universal Law of Attraction" We attract into our lives the energy and vibration we send out into the Universe. If we are sending out energy of being lonely, then the Universe will gladly give this back to us so be very careful of the thoughts, words and energy you are putting out.

Chapter 9

Antagonistic Relationship

I want you to think about someone you have an antagonistic relationship with. What would God think about you as you think about this person? What if God thought the same way about us as we often think about other people? Remember God doesn't play favorites. He loves us all equally. Serving others is the best way to help yourself. Most people only think about their own problems and yet helping others is the best way to rid yourself of problems.

Genuinely serving and helping others from your heart without expecting anything in return changes your problems into love. Be gentle, kind, patient and remember God is with you at all times. Even in the most difficult relationships, where a person did bad things in the past can be transformed in the present through one choice, one decision at a time.

The future is not fixed. Our past lives manifest as feelings and insights. When we meet someone how we feel about the person comes from our subconscious memory, our likes and dislikes from a past life. Our present manifests as whatever experiences we are currently involved in and whatever relationship we are trying to deal with. Wherever you are right now can be a purposeful experience if you choose to make it so. There is a reason why the Universe has pulled all these experiences together for you at this moment. It is because there is something you can learn to become a better person. The Universe is constantly pulling our thoughts, choices and decisions from the past into the present. You can look at the future in one of three ways: as a victim; a bystander; or a conscious co-creator. Keep in mind we are not always co-creating consciously.

Sometimes we unconsciously create our future. Very few people would knowingly create their future as a victim, but victim consciousness has become very popular in our society. In many ways we are slowly creating an entitlement culture instead of taking responsibility for our own actions and decisions. We first look to blame others for what we think they have done to us.

This is where we see inner and outer changes happening in the world or in our own life as happening to us. We have to understand that the problems life throws at us are meant to teach us lessons that we need to learn to help us grow. Problems are like waves in the ocean they continuously come at us large and small.

We all have problems. No one is immune to them, so we have to move away from the feeling that the Universe is somehow out to get us. Victim consciousness in this country is skyrocketing. An example of victim consciousness would be, you're at a restaurant and having a cup of coffee which is very hot and you burn yourself. Instead of saying I should have waited and let the coffee cool down before drinking it, you instead call a lawyer and sue the restaurant for not warning you the coffee was hot. I often hear people blaming attorneys for our trend toward an entitlement society. Don't blame the lawyers; blame the part of us that shirks personal responsibility.

When you look in the phone book or do an internet search, you'll find more listings for attorneys than for restaurants or retail stores because of victim consciousness. Today with all the political correctness in society, we need to watch everything we say because of possibly offending someone and being attacked on social media. We have lost our sense of responsibility. We always feel it is someone else's fault instead of looking in the mirror at ourselves first.

We are responsible for our own actions and decisions, no one else. Many people are bystanders because they feel we are on the verge of a new world order of peace, brotherhood, spiritual growth and transformation, and all they have to do is wait for it to happen. People feel if they live long enough they'll wake one day and there will be world peace, a clean environment and global harmony.

In reality, this holding pattern is simply not doing anything to bring about a new world order. In other words, the person is a bystander. When we consciously co-create with the Universe, we are very much aware that every thought we have, every word we speak, and every action we take is somehow creating the tomorrow we are going to experience. The external world is merely a reflection of what we've worked on or not worked on in the course of our lives.

We are all part of God and, as a co-creator, what you think and what you do – your thoughts, ideas, and actions with other people – are constantly co-creating the future. Make no mistake we need to accept responsibility for the world we are creating because we are coming back again. What kind of world do you want to come back to?

We co-create with the Universe one choice, one decision at a time. However, in spite of that, we can see glimpses of the future through our perceptions. Each of us perceives something in another person which is very specific to our own needs and development. In other words, we need to learn how to love everyone, because in the process we become a better person for having had the opportunity to be around all the other people in our lives.

Being connected to spirit is very important in relationships because it puts you in a state of wonder and unconditional love where you are not judging other people but rather just witnessing them loving their beautiful spirit. When you love and accept yourself unconditionally you are then sending loving vibration out to others. You are creating loving relationships and helping to heal the planet. Not being connected to spirit is having no intention for your life, it is like going to a movie complex, randomly buying a ticket and watching whatever movie you happen to go into.

This is how our lives work without being connected to spirit we are trying to control daily events the way our ego and intellect sees them. This never creates happiness or good relationships. On the other hand, by being connected to spirit you are setting an intention for your life, you really get a sense of where you are headed; you are inspired and apply the lessons you have learned along your journey.

I don't' set goals because they do not ultimately help us in our soul growth nor do they make us happy and fulfilled. The reason I say this is because when you set a goal you do whatever you have to do to achieve it no matter what the cost. Often when you set a goal very little thought is given as to why are you really setting the goal and if the goal you are setting is what you really want.

Once you achieve the goal you have set, there is no time to enjoy it because you are immediately setting another one and then another one. It is like a treadmill you are constantly on and can never get off. We are taught by society this is what you need to do in order to become successful.

Whereas setting an intention is a destination you intend to get to, a journey. You set your plan to make your intention happen, put in the your 50% of the work to help it manifest and then take your foot of the gas and let the Universe take over from there.

This is the key, letting the Universe take over. We live in such an ego and intellect driven society that we never want to give up control. It's amazing, once we have done our part and allow the Universe to take over how miracles happen in our lives. The journey is much more enjoyable, and the end result is far better than we could have ever accomplished by ourselves.

I am not saying not to set goals. They are important, but goals should be set as part of your overall intention. For example, if your intention is to take a trip across country, then you can set goals for the things you want to see and places you want to visit along the way.

Having intentions can help you make sense of who you really are and why you are here. You are inspired to follow your intention and spirit moves you in the right direction to live your purpose and reach your destiny. Don't overlook how important having intention is in all of your activities.

Chapter 10

Change your Future

The future is ever changing because of the vital role free will plays in our lives. Nothing is predestined or set. The soul has tendencies, urges and talents. Although these urges sometimes will push us in a certain direction, the outcome of our lives is totally connected to free will.

There are two constant factors determining our future:

The soul is destined to grow from past experiences and eventually awaken to the awareness of its relationship with, and eventual connection with spirit. Whatever it takes to bring about this growth in consciousness and connect with spirit is what the Universe will draw towards the soul.

Individuals will continue to draw a particular lesson towards them until they have learned it.

In setting our future, we must understand this distinction: God gives us the free will to decide when we learn our lessons but not if we will learn them. It's our choice as to how many lifetimes we want to repeat in order to learn those lessons.

Often, we look upon the world situation and it's all too easy to feel helpless in regards to whether or not we can have an effect upon the future of the planet. In the face of such insurmountable difficulties, what can one person possibly do? First, know wherever we find ourselves, there's work to be done. Its work that's catered to our previous experiences and skills God wants us to do in order to bring about the eventual transformation of every single soul. Some people think they are too old to pursue the future they've always wanted. Yet regardless of our age, there is always something we can do to make a positive difference in the world and transform ourselves in the process.

First thing every morning and several times throughout the day I will say, "Divine Spirit move me. Move my mind to make the right decisions. Move my feet in the right direction. Move my lips to say the right words." I then listen in quiet meditation. It doesn't matter how busy I am or how my day is going, I make time to do this.

I then act, following the direction where guidance is moving me so I can best serve. Make the world a better place because you have lived in it. You can only do this by the being in the present moment of every hour and every day.

Remember no one is promised tomorrow, the past is gone and the future has not yet arrived. Live one day at a time. Each day is a gift, be grateful for it. Never tempt it or take it for granted.

Chapter 11

It is What You Think

Very often we underestimate the power of our own thoughts. Our thoughts are either positive or negative. Since our mind can only hold one thought at a time, it's our choice what type of thought we hold in our mind. Our thoughts not only affect us but others as well. Our positive thoughts build and create a bright future whereas negative thoughts can actually cause all types of problems in the future including with our health. So the next time you feel anger or disgust towards another person, try to transform it into something more positive.

What energy or thought can you send to another person to affect a positive change in the situation rather than enabling the negativity to continue? Life is an ongoing adventure of purposeful experiences and relationships enabling individuals to find their true self. Deep within each soul there is a compelling force guiding every individual to discover who they are.

In essence, we are all seekers, pursuing our true identity and our relationship to the whole. All too often we seek meaning in our lives through escape, acquisition, addiction and judgment. At some time in our journey, we will realize we are all souls simply seeking to reconnect with source. What does the future have in store for us? Inevitably, the future contains those relationships we have found challenging, the unfinished business we continue to put off until tomorrow and the same difficulties we have repeatedly overlooked or refused to deal with. At the same time, our future will include our own transformation and connection to God. The Universe is continually molding and shaping our future with complete objectivity and flawless precision by putting us in the circumstances and events which will enable us to arrive at our destiny. It's simply a matter of our own free will as to how long it will take us to get there.

Wherever we find ourselves in the present, the situation has the potential to be a purposeful experience. Each of us enters the experience for a reason whether we choose to use the present as a positive learning experience is a matter of free will. Our future is not dependent upon what we know but rather how well we apply what we know. Chinese philosopher and poet, Lao Tzu once said, "We need to do what we know to do and the next step will be given." Often times there are tasks in our lives where we know what to do but we either have fears about doing them or we don't know how to pull off what we hope to accomplish.

Chapter 12

Have Faith

Sometimes in our life we find ourselves at a point of hopelessness where we feel we have done all that we can. It is at this point where we have to have faith. My definition of faith is releasing your personal effort and letting go of your ego, in the process you surrender your personal power to the Universe to take over. This is difficult for most people to do because we live most of our lives in our ego where we have to be in control of our decisions and the timing of them as well.

You are like a farmer, planting the seed, cultivating it, watering, and protecting it. However, you don't make the seed grow. You simply set up the conditions for the Universe to grow the seed through you. Allow the Universe to orchestrate for you, knowing you have done your part. This is faith. You must have confidence in the future based on what you've already done in the past, but if you haven't done your part, faith won't do it for you.

The Universe has its own wisdom, its own timing, its own order to events and if we second guess and continue to allow our ego to force our life in the direction we want it to go we will often sabotage and undo the good we have done especially in our relationships.

We live in a world of wanting instant gratification, but we must have patience in how we want our life to go and get out of our intellect and instead, learn to make decisions from our heart which then allows us to go with the Universal flow of God. By shifting your awareness from your intellect and into the heart you will be able to feel all is well in a deep intuitive way and wait patiently for providence.

Final Thoughts

The English author Samuel Butler, wrote "All animals except man know that the principle business of life is to enjoy it." The key to happiness and fulfillment in every area of our life is right relationships. If our relationships are not good, it will throw everything else in life off.

Our relationships are meant to help us grow and become whole. People will come and go in our life, some relationships will last a lifetime some are very short, but they all have a purpose. Every person comes into our life for a reason, to teach us important lessons we need to learn in order to grow.

Our purpose in life is to create. Since we are all connected together in our soul journey, we cannot create anything meaningful for ourselves without having good relationships. If our relationships aren't right, we will always have the feeling of things not being quite right in our life no matter what we do.

By learning from people in our lives, we can adjust inward and outward so our inner happiness is optimized and every action we take will be spontaneous from within. Happiness is very fleeting for most of us but when we have right relationships our lives can be transformed and we can have the bliss that is our birthright.

Appendix A

Resources

Free Newsletter

Would you like to receive informative articles that can help you connect with your spirit and reach advanced states of consciousness? Sign up for my email newsletter. It's free and packed with practical tools and techniques you can use to develop your intuitive abilities and then use this natural gift to expand your awareness and reconnect with your higher self. In addition, this monthly newsletter provides strategies for living a happier, more fulfilling and balanced life.

To sign up for my newsletter go to: www.joeloveiw.com

Consultations

I will guide and mentor you through a personal consultation. In our time spent together, I will reveal your soul plan, your soul's purpose, your soul lessons, and address obstacles you are currently facing. Then we will look at where you are today and how you can best align with your life's plan, overcome your blocks and get into the grace and flow immediately. The result is a quick solution and return to a peace you want and deserve.

Once you are shown how to align with your soul plan, you will be relieved of stress, wasted time and of fear so you will be able to return to your most authentic spirit and be able to live as you want.

To Schedule a 30 or 60 minute reading go to www.joeloveiw.com or **call 866-212-0608**

Seminars and Workshops

I will conduct half or full day workshops on the subjects of Sixth sensory living; Working with you spirit guides; Manifesting your desires; Chakra balancing, Power of Forgiveness, and Mind/body health. My seminars and workshops can also be customized to fit your individual needs.

For more information about my workshops and seminars go to **www.joeloveiw.com** or **call 866-212-0608**

www.ingramcontent.com/pod-product-compliance
Lightning Source LLC
Chambersburg PA
CBHW041800040426
42447CB00005B/274